"How eBook Readers are Killing Consumers' Rights"

The DMCA Promotes eBook Reader Platform DRM Technology at the Expense of Copyright Owners and Consumers

ABSTRACT:

The purchase of an eBook on restrictive eBook reader platforms only grants the customer a revocable license to view it. To ensure that the customer cannot violate her eBook license, content owners implement Digital Rights Management (DRM) technology to control and protect their works. The Digital Millennium Copyright Act of 1998 (DMCA) criminalizes any act that circumvents DRM technology. Platforms owners, like Apple and Amazon, are currently using licensing agreements, DRM technology, and patents to control copyrighted content. Through licensing, platforms are able to restrict a consumers' fair use and first-sale defense rights under copyright law. Through DRM technology, platforms are able to enforce their licenses and add restrictions that have nothing to do with copyright protection, but severely limit copyright owners' and consumers rights. Through patents, platforms seek the ability to control the resale transactions of eBooks. Through licensing agreements, DRM technology, and patents platforms have gained more power over copyrighted works than ever intended under our copyright laws.

This book proposes an amendment for the DMCA to mandate that all eBook reader platforms that implement DRM technology provide a universal format file for the reading and storage of purchases. A universal format for reading and storage of purchased files would be in accordance with the first-sale doctrine and allow for fair-use exemptions. It provides consumers fair use access to their eBook licenses by allowing them to access their purchases through different platforms. It will make the first-sale defense in the digital sphere relevant by allowing all purchases to be platform agnostic. A universal format protects copyright owners' rights by allowing their copyrighted works to be converted onto other platforms. Furthermore, it can assist patents in governing secondary markets by making the eBook technology more interoperable and the secondary market more liquid. It can also be effective at combatting privacy through "watermarking" and authentication programs. A universal format file specifically for the reading and storage of purchases would be a compromise regarding DRM technology, as copyright owners could still implement DRM technology to limit printing and copying of eBooks if so desired.

Table of Contents

I.   Introduction 3

II. The Case of the eBook 8

   A.   The Rise of the eBook 9

   B.   Platform Restrictions on eBooks 11

III.   Copyright Law 13

   A.   The First-Sale Doctrine 14

      1.   17 USC § 109 of the Copyright Act of 1976 14

      2.   *Bobbs-Merrill Co. v. Straus* 14

      3.   The Policy behind the First-Sale Doctrine 15

   B.   DMCA 16

      1.   The "Anti-Circumvention Provisions" of the DMCA 17

   C.   Digital Rights Management (DRM) technology............18

IV. A Universally Fair Format for Reading and Storage of eBooks 20

   A.   A Universal Format Provides Consumers Fair Use Access in eBook Licenses 21

   B. A Universal Format Makes the First-sale Defense in the Digital Sphere Relevant...23

   C. A Universal Format Protects Copyright Owners' and Consumers' Rights 26

      1.   A Universal Format Protects Copyright Owners' Rights...27

      2.   A Universal Format Protects Consumers' Rights.....28

   D. A Universal Format Will Make Secondary Markets More Efficient...30

   E.   A Universal Format Can Combat Piracy 33

V. Conclusion 36

I. Introduction

How can we prevent Amazon and Apple, two of the biggest players in electronic goods, from further establishing their respective monopolies? We can start by fixing the copyright laws that apply to digital material such as eBooks.

Many people do not realize that when they purchase an eBook on an iPad, Kindle, or Nook they do not actually own it. Although eBooks and print books may be comparable in price, a consumer is not permitted to sell, lend, or give away an eBook on these platforms at their discretion. The purchase of an eBook on these platforms only grants the customer a revocable license to view it.[1]

To ensure that the customer cannot violate her eBook license, content owners implement Digital Rights Management (DRM) technology to control and protect their works. The Digital Millennium Copyright Act of 1998 (DMCA) criminalizes any act that circumvents DRM technology.[2] Once an eBook is sold through

---

[1] Andy Patrizio, *You Don't Own Your Amazon Kindle*, TECHNOLOGY GUIDE (Nov. 9, 2012), http://www.technologyguide.com/feature/you-dont-own-your-amazon-kindle-ebooks/.
[2] 17 U.S.C. § 1201.

Amazon, Amazon's DRM technology restricts it from being converted to another platform or accessed by any other method besides Kindle's programs and technology. Because Amazon's DRM technology negates all conversion options, neither the copyright owner nor the consumer can move their eBook off the Kindle platform.

Content owners (like publishing houses) may own the copyright, but platform owners (like Amazon's Kindle) use DRM technology to control the "locks" to this copyright. Amazon's ability to control the copyrighted work through DRM technology effectively limits the owners' control of their copyright and restricts consumers' legal rights to their eBooks.

Consumers are saddled with switching costs (the negative costs that a consumer incurs as a result of changing platforms) if they purchase a book on another platform, because they cannot access the remainder of their library on this new platform. Therefore, if a consumer purchases eBooks on different restrictive eBook reader platforms, then she is burdened with a separate set of digital libraries for her eBooks.

In addition, Amazon's recently issued patent[3] and Apple's recent patent application[4] for digital marketplaces will presumably grant each company ultimate power to govern any type of digital transaction in its proprietary sphere. For example, the Restriction on Transfer section of Apple's recent patent application seeks to grant Apple the power to unilaterally control when an eBook can be sold, how often, to whom, and the amount it can be sold for.[5]

Most notably, the patent gives Apple and the publisher the power to set resale prices. This allows eBook reader platforms – through licensing agreements, DRM technology, and patents – much more power than ever intended under copyright laws. In other words, platforms like Apple and Amazon want the ability to control both original sales and resale transactions of eBooks. Amazon and Apple, using the very same laws that prohibit reselling eBooks on their respective platforms, want the ability to resell eBooks and control the resale process through their licensing agreements, DRM technology, and patents.

---

[3] U.S. Patent No. 8,364,595.
[4] U.S. Patent Application No. 2013006016.
[5] U.S. Patent Application No. 2013006016.

This book analyzes the consequences of allowing restrictive eBook reader platforms coupled with patents on digital content marketplaces. I argue that the DMCA must be amended to mandate that all eBook reader platforms that implement DRM technology provide a universal format file for the reading and storage of purchases.

In 2012, the Court of Justice of the European Union (CJEU) found that where a license contemplates an indefinite right of use, it equates to a "sale." The CJEU's ruling is in contrast to many of the U.S. Courts' rulings on the same issue. Current eBook licenses grant platforms too much power to restrict consumers' rights. It is only a matter of time before the United States also finds that licenses for an indefinite right of use should be classified as sales. Until we recognize that eBook licensing agreements are really sales or decriminalize the act of "circumventing" non-essential DRM technologies, a universal format requirement for eBooks provides us with the best way to comply with current copyright laws.

This book proposes an amendment for the DMCA to mandate that all eBook reader platforms that implement DRM technology provide a universal format file for the reading and storage of purchases. A universal format for reading and storage of purchased files would be in accordance with the first-sale doctrine and allow for fair-use exemptions.

A universal format provides consumers fair use access to their eBook licenses by allowing them to access their purchases through different platforms. It will make the first-sale defense in the digital sphere relevant by allowing all purchases to be platform agnostic. It protects copyright owners' rights by allowing their copyrighted works to be converted onto other platforms. Furthermore, a universal format can assist patents in governing secondary markets by making the eBook technology more interoperable and the secondary market more liquid. It can also be effective at combatting privacy through "watermarking" and authentication programs.

It is important to note that a universal format file specifically for the reading and storage of purchases is a compromise regarding DRM technology. My proposal for universal format for the reading and storage of purchases is a compromise because a copyright owner would still have the option of using DRM technology to limit printing and copying of eBooks.

This book begins (Part II) by describing the eBooks' recent rise in popularity and the platform restrictions on eBooks. In Part III, I summarize the applicable copyright laws pertaining to eBooks and eBook reader platforms, specifically the first-sale doctrine and the DMCA. In Part IV, I develop my central thesis by explaining how a universal eBook format provides consumers with fair access to their purchases and complies with the first-sale defense in copyright. Next, I discuss how a universal format protects copyright owners' and consumers' rights. I also outline how a universal format can make the eBook secondary market more efficient and how it can combat privacy. Throughout this section, I explain my thesis and address the benefits and concerns of implementing my proposal. In Part V, I conclude that my proposed policy will benefit copyright owners and consumers as well as limit anti-competitive practices of platform owners such as Apple and Amazon.

II. The Case of the eBook

This first part of this section discusses the recent rise and popularity of the eBook. The second part of this section describes how eBook licensing agreements and platform DRM technology controls copyright content and restricts consumers' rights.

A. The Rise of the eBook

In July 2010 online bookseller Amazon.com (Amazon), one of the nation's largest booksellers, reported its second quarter sales of eBooks for its proprietary Kindle outnumbered sales of hardcover books for the first time ever.[6] In January 2011 Jeff Bezos, founder and CEO of Amazon, boasted "We had our first $10 billion quarter and . . . Kindle books have now overtaken paperback books as the most popular format on Amazon.com."[7]

The popularity of eBooks on restrictive eBook reader platforms creates a litany of copyright issues. eBook reader platforms, such as Amazon's Kindle, implement DRM technology to restrict the alienability (sale or transfer) of copyrighted works. Whereas the first-sale doctrine grants an exception to the copyright holders' distribution rights, DRM technology obviates this exception by disallowing all transfer abilities of eBooks. In other words platform DRM technology has negated all secondary transfers after purchase or original sale of an eBook.

---

[6] Claire Cain Miller, *E-Books Top Hardcovers at Amazon*, N.Y. TIMES (July 19, 2010), http://www.nytimes.com/2010/07/20/technology/20kindle.html.
[7] *Amazon.com Announces Fourth Quarter Sales up 36% to $12.95 Billion*, AMAZON (Jan. 27, 2011), http://phx.corporate-ir.net/phoenix.zhtml?c=176060&p=irol-newsArticle&ID=1521090&highlight&ref=tsm_1_tw_kin_prearn_20110127.

Furthermore, 17 U.S. Code § 107 provides for fair use exceptions to a copyright owner's exclusive rights. Fair use exceptions include "use by reproduction in copies or phonorecords or by any other means specified by that section, for purposes such as criticism, comment, news reporting, teaching (including multiple copies for classroom use), scholarship, or research, is not an infringement of copyright."[8] eBook reader platforms, such as Amazon's Kindle, prevent the ability to print or reproduce copies of any type for any reason including purposes allowed under the fair use exceptions.

The sales of eBooks now account for 30% of all book transactions.[9] Amazon is now estimated to have a 65% market share of the eBook industry, while Apple and Barnes and Noble account for the majority of the rest.[10] Although Amazon sells more than just books, many take issue with Amazon's monopolistic business practices towards the book industry.

---

[8] 17 U.S.C. § 106.
[9] Jeff Bercovici, *Amazon vs. Book Publishers, By the Numbers*, FORBES (Feb. 10, 2014), http://www.forbes.com/sites/jeffbercovici/2014/02/10/amazon-vs-book-publishers-by-the-numbers/.
[10] *Id.*

B. Platform Restrictions on eBooks

eBook platforms, such as Amazon's Kindle and Apple's iBooks, seek to control copyright content and restrict consumers' legal rights through licensing, DRM technology, and patents. Although eBooks and print books may be comparable in price, a consumer is not permitted to sell, lend, or give away an eBook on these platforms at their discretion. The purchase of an eBook on these platforms only grants the customer a revocable license to view it.[11]

To ensure that the customer cannot violate her eBook license, content owners implement Digital Rights Management (DRM) technology to control and protect their works. The Digital Millennium Copyright Act of 1998 (DMCA) criminalizes any act that circumvents DRM technology.[12]

The first-sale doctrine of copyright law grants an exception to copyright holder's *distribution rights* (17 USC § 109(a) of the Copyright Act of 1976). Under the first-sale doctrine, once a

---

[11] Andy Patrizio, *You Don't Own Your Amazon Kindle*, TECHNOLOGY GUIDE (Nov. 9, 2012), http://www.technologyguide.com/feature/you-dont-own-your-amazon-kindle-ebooks/.
[12] 17 U.S.C. § 1201.

copyrighted work is legally sold or transferred, the copyright owner's interest in the material object is exhausted.

Now Amazon and Apple, using the very same laws that prohibit reselling eBooks on their respective platforms, want to allow and control this very act via patents. For example, the Restriction on Transfer section of Apple's recent patent application gives Apple the power to unilaterally control when an eBook can be sold, how often, to whom, and the amount it can be sold for.[13] The application specifically states, "digital content item 202 may be restricted regarding to whom authorized access may be transferred, when the transfer may take place, and/or how much must be charged in order for the transfer to take place. *The restrictions may be established by publisher 110, intermediary 120, or both.*" (emphasis added)

Amazon has already received a patent on a digital marketplace.[14] Amazon's patent grants it the power to create a secondary market that would control transfers of used digital objects. This market's purpose is to regulate secondary transfers and

---

[13] U.S. Patent Application No. 20130060616.
[14] U.S. Patent No. 8,364,595.

maintain scarcity in the digital realm – by controlling how many used digital object transfers are allowed.[15] For example, a Harry Potter book may be resold five times before it becomes restricted from future sales.

Under the first-sale doctrine, once a copyrighted work is legally sold or transferred, the copyright owner's interest in the material object is exhausted. Now through licensing agreements, DRM technology, and patents platforms (like Amazon) and copyright owners (publishers) are hoping to maintain interest in the material object long after it is legally sold or transferred. Platform owners, like Apple and Amazon, are seeking much more power than ever intended under copyright laws. The next section highlights the copyright laws applicable to eBooks and eBook reader platforms.

III. Copyright Law

Art. I § 8 (8) of the Federal Constitution grants Congress the power "To promote the progress of science and useful arts, by securing for limited times to authors and inventors the exclusive right to their respective writings and discoveries."[16] 17 USC § 106

---

[15] U.S. Patent No. 8,364,595.
[16] *Bobbs-Merrill Co. v. Straus*, 210 US 339 following the previous cases of *American Tobacco Co. v. Werckmeister,* 207 U.S. 284; *White-Smith Music Co. v.*

(3) gives copyright owners the exclusive right "to distribute copies or phonorecords of the copyrighted work to the public by sale or other transfer of ownership, or by rental, lease, or lending."[17] The first-sale doctrine grants an exception to copyright holder's *distribution rights*.

A. The First-Sale Doctrine

1. 17 USC § 109 of the Copyright Act of 1976

17 USC § 109(a) of the Copyright Act of 1976 is known as the first-sale doctrine. 17 USC § 109 states "the owner of a particular copy or phonorecord lawfully made under this title, or any person authorized by such owner, is entitled, without the authority of the copyright owner, to sell or otherwise dispose of the possession of that copy or phonorecord."[18] The Court's ruling in *Bobbs-Merrill Co. v. Straus* was the nexus for the "first-sale doctrine."[19]

2. *Bobbs-Merrill Co. v. Straus*

In *Straus* the appellants, Bobbs-Merrill Company, sold the novel "The Castaway" and printed a notice on it that read "The price

---

Apollo Co., 209 U.S. 1.
[17] 17 U.S.C. § 106.
[18] 17 U.S.C. § 109.
[19] 210 US 339.

of this book at retail is one dollar net. No dealer is licensed to sell it at a less price, and a sale at a less price will be treated as an infringement of the copyright." The appellees, R.H. Macy & Co., purchased the novel wholesale and sold copies of it at retail at the price of 89 cents a copy.[20]

In this case of first impression, the Supreme Court addressed the question whether copyright law allows an owner to control a purchaser's subsequent sale of a copyrighted work.[21] The Court answered this question in the negative. The Supreme Court ruled that Bobbs-Merrill Company was not allowed to control the resale price of the novel "The Castaway" by putting a notice in the book.[22] It did not address the resale authority of licensing agreements.

3.   The Policy behind the First-Sale Doctrine

The alienability (sale or transfer) of copyrighted works and reasonable restraints on these works are the primary motivations behind the first-sale doctrine. Once the copyrighted work is legally sold or transferred, the copyright owner's interest in the material object is exhausted. However, the first-sale doctrine does not grant

---

[20] *Id.*
[21] *Id.*
[22] *Id.*

the new owner the privilege to make new copies of the original

work. The first-sale doctrine only limits the copyright owner's

distribution rights, not her *reproduction rights*.

B. DMCA

In 1998 Congress passed the DMCA, which was designed to

fight piracy by making it a felony to "circumvent" DRM technology.

The reasons that Congress passed the DMCA[23] were two-fold. As

the Efficient Frontier Foundation[24] (EFF) highlights:

> First, Congress was responding to the perceived need
> to implement obligations imposed on the U.S. by the
> 1996 World Intellectual Property Organization
> (WIPO) Copyright Treaty. Section 1201, however,
> went further than the WIPO treaty required.[25] The
> details of section 1201, then, were a response not just
> to U.S. treaty obligations, but also to the concerns of
> copyright owners that their works would be widely
> pirated in the networked digital world.[26]

---

[23] Executive Summary DMCA Section 104 Report, COPYRIGHT.GOV, *available
at* http://www.copyright.gov/reports/studies/dmca/dmca_executive.html (last
visited Dec. 7, 2014).
[24] *About EFF*, ELECTRONIC FRONTIER FOUNDATION,
https://www.eff.org/about (last visited Dec. 7, 2014).
[25] *See WIPO Copyright Treaties Implementation Act and Online Copyright
Liability Limitation Act: Hearing on H.R. 2281 and H.R. 2280 before the House
Subcomm. on Courts and Intellectual Prop.*, 105th Cong., 1st sess. (Sept. 16,
1997) at 62 (testimony of Asst. Sec. of Commerce and Commissioner of Patents
and Trademarks Bruce A. Lehman admitting that section 1201 went beyond the
requirements of the WIPO Copyright Treaty).
[26] For a full description of the events leading up to the enactment of the DMCA,
see Jessica Litman, Digital Copyright 89-150 (2000).

Section 1201 contains two distinct prohibitions: a ban on *acts* of circumvention, and a ban on the *distribution of tools and technologies* used for circumvention.

1. The "Anti-Circumvention Provisions" of the DMCA

The second part of the DMCA, 17 U.S. Code § 1201, further expands copyright protections and makes it a federal criminal offense to unscramble encrypted content or circumvent DRM technology without the copyright owner's permission.[27] The second part of the DMCA is commonly known as the "anti-circumvention provisions." In regards to circumvention of copyright protection systems, 17 U.S. Code § 1201 states:

> (a) (1) (A) No person shall circumvent a technological measure that effectively controls access to a work protected under this title... (2) No person shall manufacture, import, offer to the public, provide, or otherwise traffic in any technology, product, service, device, component, or part thereof, that— (A) is primarily designed or produced for the purpose of circumventing protection afforded by a technological measure that effectively protects a right of a copyright owner under this title in a work or a portion thereof; (B) has only limited commercially significant purpose or use other than to circumvent protection afforded by a technological measure that effectively protects a right of a copyright owner under this title in a work or a portion thereof; or (C) is

---

[27] 17 U.S.C. § 506.

marketed by that person or another acting in concert with that person with that person's knowledge for use in circumventing protection afforded by a technological measure that effectively protects a right of a copyright owner under this title in a work or a portion thereof.[28]

Furthermore the second part of the DMCA, 17 U.S. Code § 1201, "does not provide for a fair use exemption and noticeably lacks a scienter requirement."[29] The lack of defenses in the DMCA certainly provides fodder for "aggressive plaintiffs to prevent competition and interoperability."[30]

C. Digital Rights Management (DRM) technology

The DMCA makes it a felony to "circumvent" copyright-protection schemes such as DRM technology. The United States Patent and Trademark Office (USPTO) has stated that DRM technology permits "content owners to assert much finer-grained control over digital media – embodying copyrighted works, authenticating users and the integrity of content, and developing new business models for digital content in addition to simply deterring piracy."[31]

---

[28] 17 U.S.C. § 1201.
[29] Band, Jonathan and Katoh, Masanobu (2011). *Interfaces on Trial 2.0*. MIT Press. p. 92. ISBN 978-0-262-01500-4.
[30] *Id.*

The EFF argues that there is no actual evidence that DRM technology fulfills its stated purposes – to fight copyright infringement online and keep consumers safe from viruses. The EFF states "DRM has proliferated thanks to the DMCA of 1998, which sought to outlaw any attempt to bypass DRM."[32]

The American Library Association[33] raises several concerns regarding DRM technology:

- **Eliminating the "First sale" doctrine** – by limiting the secondary transfer of works to others.
- **Enforcing a "Pay-per-use" model of information dissemination** – that, if it becomes the dominant or even sole mode of access, will be contrary to the public purposes of copyright law.
- **Enforcing time limits or other limitations of use that prevent preservation and archiving** – Many market models of DRM distribution systems envision content that essentially disappears after a specific period of time or number of uses. DRM technologies can also prevent copying content into new formats.
- **Eliminating "fair use" and other exceptions in Copyright Law that underpin education,**

---

[31] *Technological Protection Systems for Digitized Copyrighted Works: A Report to Congress*, USPTO, *available at*
 http://www.uspto.gov/web/offices/dcom/olia/teachreport.pdf (last visited Dec. 7, 2014).
[32] *DRM*, ELECTRONIC FRONTIER FOUNDATION,
https://www.eff.org/issues/drm (last visited Dec. 7, 2014).
[33] *About ALA*, AMERICAN LIBRARY ASSOCIATION,
http://www.ala.org/aboutala/ (last visited Dec. 7, 2014).

criticism, and scholarship - DRM technology can prevent normal uses of works protected by copyright law, such as printing or excising portions for quotation.[34]

In the next section, I discuss the most controversial copyright issues regarding eBooks and why a universal format for the reading and storage of eBooks makes sense.

IV. A Universally Fair Format for Reading and Storage of eBooks

This section outlines my thesis and explains how platforms use licensing, DRM technology, and patents to control copyright content and restrict consumers' rights under copyright law.

In response, I propose a universal format that provides a fair resolution for copyright owners and consumers by allowing copyright owners to maintain control of their work and granting consumers fair access to these works. I propose that the DMCA should be amended to mandate that all eBook reader platforms that implement

---

[34] *DRM and Libraries*, AMERICAN LIBRARY ASSOCIATION, http://www.ala.org/advocacy/copyright/digitalrights (last visited Dec. 7, 2014).

DRM technology provide a universal format file for the reading and storage of purchases.

A universal format file specifically for the reading and storage of purchases would be a compromise regarding DRM technology, as copyright owners could still implement DRM technology to limit printing and copying of eBooks if so desired. A universal format for reading and storage of purchased files complies with the first-sale doctrine and allows for fair-use exemptions.

A. A Universal Format Provides Consumers Fair Use Access in eBook Licenses

A universal format for reading and storage would guarantee a consumer has fair access to their eBooks by allowing them to use alternative platforms to access their eBooks. A universal format for reading and storage complies with the first-sale doctrine and fair use exceptions. The whole premise for why consumers' rights are limited regarding eBooks is because they have entered into a license agreement rather than a sales transaction. If an eBook purchase was considered a sales transaction rather than a license agreement, then restrictive eBook reader platforms would be deemed illegal because they violate the first-sale doctrine and fair use exceptions.

The *Straus* Court failed to address the question whether a license on the first-sale of a book could create an obligation.[35] For whatever reasons, we accept that platforms, such as Apple and Amazon, are allowed to create obligations through licensing. By default, we allow restrictive platforms to contract with consumers using eBook licensing. It seems rather odd that content creators or technology platforms are allowed to control future sales simply by using the term "license" rather than "sale."

On July 3, 2012 the Court of Justice of the European Union (CJEU) held in *UsedSoft GmbH v. Oracle International Corp.,* that Oracle could not prevent the resale of copies of its software programs by UsedSoft.[36] The CJEU rejected this argument. The Court found that where a license contemplates an indefinite right of use, it equates to a "sale."[37] The CJEU's ruling is in contrast to many of the U.S. Courts' rulings on the same issue.

---

[35] 210 US 339.
[36] See Case C-128/11, *UsedSoft GmbH v. Oracle International Corp.*, 2012 EUR-Lex CE LEX LEXIS _ (July 3, 2012).
[37] *Id.*

For the alleged sake of copyright protection, we are allowing Apple's iTunes and Amazon's Kindle to sell content and label each transaction as an "indefinite license for the right of use." Just as the CJEU ruled that these licenses equate to a sale, the U.S. should rule that eBook licenses are actually a sale. Because of the inherent unfairness (to consumers) of restrictive licenses, I believe the U.S. will eventually rule that this type of license does actually constitute a sale. Until this happens, it makes sense to require a universal format.

B. A Universal Format Makes the First-sale Defense in the Digital Sphere Relevant

Copyright law allows for customers, "without the authority of the copyright owner, to sell or otherwise dispose of the possession of that copy (first-sale doctrine)."[38] Recent court rulings jeopardize the first-sale doctrine's application in the digital realm.

On March 30, 2013 in *Capitol Records, LLC v. ReDigi Inc.*, Capitol Records claimed copyright infringement against ReDigi because it provided a means to resell Apple's iTunes digital music tracks.[39] In striking down ReDigi's first-sale defense, Judge Sullivan states "a ReDigi user owns the phonorecord that was created when

---

[38] 17 U.S.C. § 109.
[39] 934 F. Supp. 2d 640.

she purchased and downloaded a song from iTunes to her hard disk. But to sell that song on ReDigi, she must produce a new phonorecord on the ReDigi server. Because it is therefore impossible for the user to sell her 'particular' phonorecord on ReDigi, the first-sale statute cannot provide a defense."[40]

Until the *Redigi* ruling is overturned, a universal format file is the optimal solution because it provides an alternate file for the consumer to sell, if resale is permitted. If a universal eBook file is required, then a consumer would not have to "produce a new" file rather they could sell this universal "particular" file on the Redigi server. It is possible that Redigi develops the proper technology to overcome this discriminatory ruling, but until then a universal format is the fairest solution.

The inherent problem with this formulistic interpretation is that it either removes the first-sale doctrine from the digital sphere or exclusively allows the original technology platform from which the "particular" file was purchased to resell it. The *Redigi* decision leads to an absurd result. It grants the restrictive platforms absolute power

---

[40] *Id.*

over copyright content by granting them the only rights to govern the commerce of the digital works.

According to the *Redigi* decision, Apple would be able to resell its content, but ReDigi is banned from the same practice. This interpretation only further ingrains consumers into restrictive platforms such as Apple's iTunes or Amazon's Kindle. Granting Apple and Amazon patents to effectively govern secondary transactions, but excluding others from doing the same (*Redigi* decision), is akin to granting them a de jure (government granted) monopoly.

In striking down ReDigi's fair use defense, Judge Sullivan found that the use of the copyrighted works was not transformative.[41] Now if authors are allowed to collude with the platform owners regarding resale pricing and terms through publisher-retailer contracts (as Apple's recent patent application[42] seeks to create), then it is unlikely that authors would have fair use concerns regarding the reselling process. As long as publishers and authors

---

[41] *Redigi*, 934 F. Supp. 2d 640.
[42] U.S. Patent Application No. 2013006016.

could profit from the reselling of their works, fair use concerns would recede.

In accordance with the *Redigi* ruling, consumers would have no first-sale defenses and alternative platforms would have no fair use exceptions. Meanwhile, recently granted and applied for patents would allow platform and copyright owners the right to govern content long after the initial sale. At the end of the day, this is about money. The reselling of digital media potentially creates a "one penny problem." If the publishers and platforms can find a way to make the reselling of digital media profitable, they will exploit it. Right now, the reselling of digital media is illegal, but in the future it will not only be legal – it will be profitable.   If Apple and Amazon are allowed to resell digital content, then a universal format file will allow companies like Redigi to do the same. Currently, Apple's and Amazon's licenses restrict the reselling of eBooks, but these licenses may soon be forced to change.

C. A Universal Format Protects Copyright Owners' and Consumers' Rights

In this section, I discuss how platform DRM technology is usurping copyright owners' rights and restricting consumers' legal rights to eBooks.

1. A Universal Format Protects Copyright Owners' Rights

By requiring a universal format, copyright owners are able to avoid non-essential platform encryption methods (DRM technology not used for copyright protection).

Once an eBook is sold through a restrictive platform, the platform's DRM technology restricts copyright owners and consumers from converting their eBook to another platform. Restrictive platform DRM technology denies consumer access to the eBook by any other method besides Kindle's programs and technology.

Cory Doctorow, author of the book "Information Doesn't Want to be Free," describes how platform owners like Amazon have usurped control of copyrighted works through the metaphor of "locks." Doctorow states:

> Under normal circumstances, if Amazon decided not to sell Hachette's books, you would expect Hachette to say to all the people who want to read J.K Rowling or Amanda Palmer's new book, "Here's a tool that lets

you convert your e-books to run on iBooks or on Google Play or on Kobo or on Nook. Go ahead and just switch to someone else's store, and buy your books there." But because only Amazon is allowed to unlock Hachette's books, even though Hachette controls the copyright, Amazon controls the lock. Amazon now runs that negotiation. They have all the negotiating leverage, and what happens is the rightful share of the investor is expropriated by the platform.[43]

Amazon's ability to control the copyrighted work through DRM technology effectively limits the owners' control of their copyright and restricts consumers' rights to their eBooks. Content owners (like publishing houses) may own the copyright, but platform owners (like Amazon's Kindle) use DRM technology to control the "locks" to this copyright.

2. A Universal Format Protects Consumers' Rights

By requiring a universal format, consumers can access their purchases through their chosen platform. Copyright law allows for customers, "without the authority of the copyright owner, to sell or otherwise dispose of the possession of that copy (first-sale doctrine)."[44] Copyright law also allows for reproduction in copies

---

[43] *Picking The Locks: Redefining Copyright Law In The Digital Age*, NPR (Nov. 3, 2014),
http://www.npr.org/2014/11/03/360196476/picking-the-locks-redefining-copyright-law-in-the-digital-age.

"for purposes such as criticism, comment, news reporting, teaching (including multiple copies for classroom use), scholarship, or research (fair use exceptions)."[45]

The purchase of an eBook on restrictive platforms only grants the customer a revocable license to view it.[46] The DMCA grants restrictive platform DRM technology the power to restrict a consumer's ability to sell, lend, copy, or print an eBook at her discretion. In other words, licenses and DRM technology restrict consumers' rights under copyright law. Restrictive platform DRM technology unfairly negates the first-sale doctrine and fair use exceptions for eBook consumers.

Because restrictive platform DRM technology "locks" an eBook into its specific platform, consumers are not allowed to access the eBook using another platform. Consumers are saddled with switching costs (the negative costs that a consumer incurs as a result of changing platforms) if they purchase a book on another platform, because they cannot access their eBook library on this new platform.

---

[44] 17 U.S.C. § 109.
[45] 17 U.S.C. § 107.
[46] Andy Patrizio, *You Don't Own Your Amazon Kindle*, TECHNOLOGY GUIDE (Nov. 9, 2012), http://www.technologyguide.com/feature/you-dont-own-your-amazon-kindle-ebooks/.

As Matteo Berlucchi, CEO of London-based social e-retailer Anobii, warns "Amazon uses DRM to lock people in. You can't take the files out. The problem is that if you go down the Amazon road, you can't drop out. If you drop out of Kindle, you lose all your books."[47] The following section discusses a solution to restrictive platform DRM technology.

D. A Universal Format Will Make Secondary Markets More Efficient

A universal format will free consumers from the shackles of a specific platform. If a platform decides not to sell a publisher's books, then a universal format will allow consumers to move their universal formatted files to another platform and buy the publisher's book on the alternative platform. If publishers require, a universal format can still be encrypted with the DRM technology that prevents copying, printing, and sharing. When the reselling of eBooks is allowed, a universal format will help make the secondary market for eBooks more liquid.

---

[47] Jeremy Greenfield, *Bookseller Backed by Big Publishers Advocates Abandoning DRM*, DIGITAL BOOK WORLD (Jan. 25, 2012), http://www.digitalbookworld.com/2012/bookseller-backed-by-big-publishers-advocates-abandoning-digital-rights-management/.

In his New York Times article "Reselling E-Books and the One Penny Problem," David Progue highlights the "one penny problem."[48] Progue writes, "Bob buys an e-book from Amazon for $10. After reading, he sells it to a new person for $8. After a couple more transactions the used e-book is going for $1. . . With unlimited e-book sales, every book's price would eventually drop to a penny." [49]

Amazon already owns a patent for a digital marketplace[50] and Apple has applied for a patent on a digital marketplace as well.[51] As Progue point out, "These patents also give the publisher or bookstore the right to impose a minimum price for reselling an e-book. . . . Both proposals suggest that publishers could also limit the number of times a digital item can be resold. . . These thresholds help to maintain scarcity of digital objects in the marketplace."[52]

Many would point out that an unrestricted universal format would haphazardly increase supply in the eBook marketplace. An

[48] David Progue, *Reselling E-Books and the One Penny Problem*, N.Y. TIMES (March 14, 2013), http://pogue.blogs.nytimes.com/2013/03/14/reselling-e-books-and-the-one-penny-problem/.
[49] *Id.*
[50] U.S. Patent No. 8,364,595.
[51] U.S. Patent Application No. 20130060616.
[52] David Progue, *Reselling E-Books and the One Penny Problem*, N.Y. TIMES (March 14, 2013), http://pogue.blogs.nytimes.com/2013/03/14/reselling-e-books-and-the-one-penny-problem/.

unrestricted format is not what I am advocating for. Many people may be skeptical of a universal format with proper encryption technology to prevent unfettered copying and printing, but it is possible. The encryption technology is already being used to limit copying and printing. There is no reason why a universal format could not incorporate these restrictions.

A universal format embedded with essential copyright-protecting DRM technology makes sense. A universal format strictly for reading and storage strikes the proper balance between abusive DRM technology that severely limits consumers' rights and unrestricted access to copyrighted material that results in the "one penny problem" as well as piracy problems. A universal format will not change the inevitable future of digital sales. It is only a matter of time before we allow the reselling of digital media. However, a universal format file will limit the absolute power we have granted restrictive platforms through licensing, DRM technology, and patents (current and pending).

E. A Universal Format Can Combat Piracy

In Jaqueline Lipton's article "Copyright, Plagiarism, and Emerging Norms in Digital Publishing," she states "One solution to some of the problems inherent in the digital piracy area is to put more pressure – legal or otherwise – on the leading online distribution platforms for digital books to ensure that they have transparent and accessible practices in place to combat digital piracy."[53] For the sake of piracy protection, copyright owners have ceded control of their content to platform owners like Apple and Amazon. We are only now witnessing the unintended consequences of granting platforms this type of power.

Many claim that DRM technology is the best way to protect against piracy. But as we saw in 2007, when the majority of the music industry dropped DRM technology, there was no evidence of any increase in music piracy. In reality, restrictive platforms use DRM technology to prevent competition by restricting access to eBooks purchased on its format. These platforms use DRM technology to restrict interoperability by forcing content owners and consumers to exclusively use their format and blocking each party's ability to convert an eBook into another format. The platform DRM

---

[53] Jacqueline Lipton, *Copyright, Plagiarism, and Emerging Norms in Digital Publishing.* VANDERBILT JOURNAL OF ENTERTAINMENT AND TECHNOLOGY LAW, 16(3), at 585, *available at* http://go.galegroup.com/ps/i.do?id=GALE%7CA374695869&v=2.1&u=lom_acce ssmich&it=r&p=AONE&sw=w&asid=5022eced8a2bc7a2f55a5972515c35d4.

technology effectively grants a key to platform owners that locks copyrighted work on its platform. Only the platform owner can unlock the copyrighted work.

A universal format can also protect eBooks against piracy. One method a universal format could implement is called "watermarking." For example, an eBook could have the original purchaser's information on the top corner of all its pages, essentially tagging or embedding the copyrighted work so that each file is attributed to a specific customer. In fact, author J.K. Rowling already uses "watermarking," rather than DRM technology, to protect her Harry Potter eBook series against piracy. By avoiding restrictive DRM technology, customers can purchase eBooks directly from her and read them on any platform.

A universal format could also limit access to purchased-material through simple authentication methods such as username and password programs. It could prevent copying and printing through encryption technology that is already widely implemented in the industry. A universal format is not an all-or-nothing proposition regarding DRM technology; it is a compromise. Remember, I am only proposing a universal format for reading and storage – not copying or printing. These options, as well as others, are still left to the copyright owners. As further evidence that a universal format would not substantially harm the eBook market, universal formats such as Epub and PDF already exist. Kobo, Sony Reader, and Google Play are all universal eBook-reader platforms that have adopted the Epub format.

An alternative view to my proposal is that strategies like "watermarking" and authentication programs are still nascent methods of protecting eBooks against piracy. There is always substantial risk when adopting new technologies and this should be accounted for when proposing a reduction in DRM technology protections. Furthermore, although there are universal formats out there, they do not currently have a substantial market share. It is still too early to tell if a universal format would harm the eBook market; there is simply not enough data to analyze the effects of a universal format. Many copyright owners prefer DRM technology to combat privacy because they believe it has been tested and works. As of now, other methods of combatting privacy have simply not proven to be as effective as DRM technology.

Taking this all into consideration, I still believe a universal eBook format specifically for the reading and storage of purchase is an optimal solution. A universal format requires platform DRM technology to better comply with existing copyright laws by limiting non-essential (non-copyright protecting) mechanisms that severely limit consumers' legal rights to eBooks. This proposal makes more sense than allowing current DRM technology to obviate the first-sale doctrine and fair use exceptions from the digital realm.

V. Conclusion

Until we recognize that eBook licensing agreements are really sales or decriminalize the act of "circumventing" non-essential DRM technologies, a universal format requirement for eBooks provides us with the best way to comply with current copyright laws. It is only a matter of time before the "one penny problem" is solved and we allow for the reselling of digital media.

When this happens, platforms like Apple and Amazon – through licensing agreements, DRM technology, and patents – will control copyrighted works in a way copyright law never imagined or meant to allow.

In response, I propose a universal format for reading and storage that allows copyright owners to maintain control of their work and grants consumers fair access to these works. A universal format for reading and storage of purchased files would be in accordance with the first-sale doctrine and allow for fair-use exemptions. It provides consumers fair use access to their eBook licenses by allowing them to access their purchases through different platforms. It will make the first-sale defense in the digital sphere relevant by allowing all purchases to be platform agnostic.

A universal format protects copyright owners' rights by allowing their copyrighted works to be converted onto other platforms. Furthermore, it can assist patents in governing secondary markets by making the eBook technology more interoperable and the secondary market more liquid. It can also be effective at combatting privacy through "watermarking" and authentication programs. A universal format is not an all-or-nothing proposition regarding DRM technology; it is a compromise. Remember, I am only proposing a universal format for reading and storage – not copying or printing. These options, as well as others, may still be left to the discretion of copyright owners.

The more we use technology to protect our rights, the more at risk we are of becoming prisoners of this technology. A fair balance between copyright owners, eBook reader platforms, and consumer rights is necessary for the proper evolution of the eBook industry.

www.ingramcontent.com/pod-product-compliance
Lightning Source LLC
Chambersburg PA
CBHW071020180526
45168CB00003B/1504